RAVENNA

Antonio Paolucci

RAVENNA

Constable
London

CONTENTS

© 1971 SCALA, Istituto Fotografico Editoriale
Color photographs: SCALA, Florence
Monochrome photographs: Alinari, Anderson, Scala
Layout: Leone Sbrana
Translation: Simon Dally
Produced by SCALA, Istituto Fotografico Editoriale
Printed in Italy by coop. officine grafiche firenze. 1978

RAVENNA

HISTORY

Inhabited by the Umbrians and probably colonized by the Etruscans, Ravenna was already in existence several centuries before Christianity. On this point ancient writers are as much in agreement as modern scholars. But by the second century B.C., along with the whole of the Po Valley north of Rimini, Ravenna had fallen to the Romans, who changed the city into a commercial center of great strategic importance. In his colossal military and political reorganization of the Roman Empire, the Emperor Augustus fortified the rear of the city with a system of canals which bound it to the Po; he built the large port of Classis and made it the base of one of the best-equipped fleets of the Empire. At this time the praetorian fleet of Classis comprised an impressive number of warships; the naval command of Ravenna controlled the Adriatic trade routes and was responsible for keeping the peace in the Eastern Provinces.

A period of continuous growth began for Ravenna which reached its zenith in the fifth century when, under the force of exceptional circumstances, the Adriatic city was designated by command of the Emperor Honorius to replace Milan as capital of the Christian and Roman Empire of the West. In the widespread fragmentation of the Roman Empire, brought about by successive invasions of barbarian tribes and the constant threat of military insurrection, Ravenna, protected in the rear by its ring of canals and marshes which made it virtually impregnable, and defended on the seaward side by its strategically placed port, enjoyed peculiar advantages. However, none of this could prevent the rapid crumbling of the Empire; in 476 the power of Rome came to an end with the overthrow of Romulus Augustulus, and the barbarian Odoacre assumed the title King of Italy. He in turn was soon ousted, in 493, by the Ostrogoth Theodoric. For more than thirty years, until his death in 526, King Theodoric ruled wisely over a people of barbarian and Arian origins. (The followers of Arius were in opposition to the Nicaean Catholic orthodoxy on the question of the human nature of Christ.) During this period a number of notable buildings were added to the city, and its defenses were strengthened. Theodoric tried, at least in the first part of his reign, to foster an atmosphere of tolerance and understanding with the local population, which was Latin and Catholic. In 540, after one of the most savage wars in history, the forces of the Byzantine general Belisarius entered the city. Annihilated, the Goths disappeared forever from the scene. Italy and the West once more became provinces of the Eastern Empire and, for a short while, it looked as if the political and cultural unity of the world had been resurrected. But Justinian's great dream was bound to fail, for no amount of political control could keep the West and East together for any length of time.

For the next two centuries it fell to Ravenna to keep alive the appearance of Imperial power, and to continue the tradition of classical art in a country overrun with barbarians and convulsed by vast ethnic and cultural upheavals. The name of Romagna (land of the Romans), which the territory around Ravenna still bears today, shows the consciousness its inhabitants had, during the dark centuries of the Middle Ages, that they were the last island of civilization amidst a sea of barbarians. When, in 751, the city was occupied by the Longobards and the last Byzantine exarch abandoned it, Ravenna's great history was virtually over. Even the sources of its former prosperity dried up. The port of Classis, unused and neglected, silted up and today no longer exists; the waters, no longer controlled by the Roman canal system, became marshes; and the state of the economy deteriorated to the extent that, from having been an industrial sea-power, the city now depended upon farming and fishing to maintain itself. During the feudal age of Commune government, Ravenna's pre-

stige declined still further. In the field of culture the neighbouring city of Bologna, with its famous *Studio*, took over the rôle which had once belonged to the city of the exarchs, while the Adriatic little by little came under Venetian rule. In 1431 the Republic of Venice took direct control over Ravenna and held it until the beginning of the sixteenth century, at which time the whole of Romagna passed into the hands of the Church. For more than 300 years the ancient capital of the West was reduced to the rank of a large outlying village, so bereft of any artistic and cultural life of its own that from the seventeenth to the eighteenth century Ravenna failed to produce a single artist of note. The only important work of art of the Baroque period surviving in the city is the cycle of frescoes which decorate the Chapel of the Blessed Sacrament in the Cathedral. Even these are the work of a « foreigner » — the Bolognese artist Guido Reni, with the assistance of pupils. Through the whole first half of the nineteenth century Ravenna continued to be one of the poorest and least significant provinces of North Italy, and only after the country's unification did it begin slowly to recover its strength. Today, due to the reclaiming of land which took place at the end of the last century, and to the remarkable expansion which has occurred in its industry and docks since the last war, Ravenna is experiencing a period of great prosperity and is regaining, at least in some measure, her traditional rôle — vital during her brief period of artistic glory — of gateway to the Balkans and the eastern Mediterranean.

No consideration of Early Christian and Byzantine Ravenna can fail to begin with the Mausoleum of Galla Placidia. In spite of its small size there is no doubt that this little church, which has the shape of a Latin cross, is the most outstanding fifth-century monument in Ravenna. However, it is extremely unlikely that the building did in fact house the remains of the famous daughter of Emperor Theodosius I, Galla Placidia, who, after marrying first the barbarian Emperor Ataulfo and then the patrician Constance III, ruled Ravenna and the West for many years as Empress and later as regent in the name of her son, Valentinian III. It is known that Galla Placidia died in Rome in 450, and she was probably buried there. The Mausoleum which she had built some twenty years earlier was never to receive her mortal remains, nor those of Constance, her husband, nor her brother Honorius, even if this had been her original intention.

The building, which has now sunk some four feet into the ground, is extremely simple: attached to a rather low, square central tower are the four arms, each with a sloping roof overhanging a pediment. Each pediment is subtly emphasized by brick moldings. Blind arches all around the brick walls effect a gentle play of light over the surface, thus breaking the regularity of the building's neatly ordered exterior.

In contrast to the outside, the interior of the Mausoleum is astonishingly rich in decoration. The cupola, which is placed under the roof of the central tower, the barrel-vaults hidden externally by the other four roofs, the lunettes on the end walls, and the large lunettes which weld the arms of the cross to the cupola, are completely covered with mosaics. The lower part of the walls is faced with yellow marble, while the light filters in through fourteen windows made of extremely thin sheets of alabaster. The decorations were conceived and executed as a single entity and they all focus on the Christian idea of redemption, a theme which emphasizes the original purpose of the Mausoleum. The cupola itself is covered with gold stars set in concentric circles against a dark blue background, and it is dominated by the figure of the Cross, representing the idea of the eternal and triumphant Christ. This is the focal point both of the mosaic decorations and the architecture itself. In the corners of the cupola, the four symbols of the Evangelists stand out, executed in gold tesserae in order to leave no doubt as to their heavenly meaning; the effect is that of an almost mystical radiation pouring from the bearers of God's word in a shimmer of gold and blue over the surrounding decorations. Immediately below, sharply defined against the deep blue background, are the figures of eight Apostles, placed in pairs in the four large lunettes which bound the drum of the cupola, above each pair a canopy in the shape of a large shell. The only two figures who are distinguishable from the others are St. Peter and St. Paul. All wear flowing white togas and have their right hands raised in the typical gesture of acclamation of Roman senators. That they descend from classical models, from Roman statuary, is in fact quite obvious. At their feet are two doves, one approaching a fountain, the other bending its neck to drink. This is an allusion to the souls who approach the visible Church of Jesus Christ: water of the True Faith and the Life Eternal.

A very similar idea is expressed in the side lunettes; in these, two pairs of stags, deep in an entanglement of acanthus, slake their thirst in the blue waters of a pool, symbolizing the eternal longing of the spirit for the divine spring of faith. Above, in the hollow of the two barrel-vaults, among the branches of the vine ("I am the vine, ye are the branches..." John XV.5), as if to confirm the spiritual significance of the twin motif, shines the "Signum Christi", the primal symbol of Christianity in the first centuries. Finally, in the lunette on the far wall, and in the one above the entrance, two themes are depicted which fit in perfectly with the rest of the decorations: the triumph of Faith which overcomes every trial, in the figure of Deacon Lawrence who goes joyfully to his martyrdom on the flaming gridiron, and the merciful care of Christ, seen as the Good Shepherd watching over his sheep.

Thus the overall iconographical plan of Galla Placidia presents a series of important religious concepts which, though evolved within a complicated theological context, are expressed with extraordinary simplicity and clarity. The process of making figures more abstract and the increasing intellectualization of the content, which from the sixth century on enveloped Western art, ending the Hellenistic-Roman tradition and laying the foundations for the birth of a new artistic language, had not yet touched the mosaicists who worked on the Mausoleum of Galla Placidia. They still display, in a pure, straight forward style, an archetypal vocabulary of colors and form which are in the unbroken tradition of classical art.

It is difficult to know whether the team of artists who executed these outstanding mosaics, from around 425 to 430, came from Rome, Syria, or Constantinople, and this is not the place to discuss the various reasons scholars give in support of one theory or another; the important thing is that these great and unfortunately unknown artists undoubtedly drew their inspiration from the most sophisticated works of ancient art. The astonishing range of colors, the variety and elegance of the decoration, the logic of the iconographical scheme with its lofty concepts — all these come directly from the classical world. Above all there is the natural quality of the pictures. Let us consider for example the beautiful scene showing the stags by the spring: the idea which this expresses does not in the least lead the artist into producing a stylized or abstract picture, but on the contrary inspires him to depict naturalistic elements in a fresh and purely poetic manner. The colors of the plants are soft and varied; the waters of the mystic pool ripple; the thirsty animals with their dappled hides and gilded throats and bellies seem to quiver with life, while the lighter color of the mosaic around their feet gives a strong impression of depth. In the same way the idea of Christ as the guardian of the mystic flock, in the lunette of the Good Shepherd, is expressed almost completely naturalistically: the rocky landscape, skilfully broken up, fills the empty space and gives the scene depth; the blue sky, which is lighter in the center, gives a hint of perspective. The shadows stand out clearly on the ground;

the different plants, and the animals which are all seen in different poses, reflect the variety and truth of the physical world. The same applies to the other scenes in the Mausoleum: even the purely decora- tive elements, in the pagan joyfulness of their colors and the naturalism of their details, reveal a determination typical of classical art to place idealized concepts and abstract ideas in a physical context.

Mausoleum of
Galla Placidia
Exterior

In contrast to the Mausoleum of Galla Placidia, which in its humble appearance and modest dimensions can almost escape notice, the Basilica of San Vitale captures one's attention at first glance. This enormous temple was built to emulate the great churches of the East, and was intended to proclaim the glories of a great capital. We know that the construction of the building was begun in 525, when Ravenna was still ruled by the Goths, and that it was consecrated in 548 when, after one of the most terrible wars in history, the whole of Italy fell under the power of Byzantium. We also know that the man who financed this gigantic project was the extremely rich Ravenna banker Giuliano Argentario, and that the final cost came to 26,000 gold pieces. But we do not know who planned the famous basilica, although he must have been one of the greatest architects of his day.

The building, plain brick on the outside, has an octagonal plan. Encircling the central section, which conceals the cupola, are two ambulatories, one above the other; the upper one; called *matroneum*, was that part of ancient Christian basilicas which was usually reserved for women. Flanking the apse are the *prothesis* and *diaconicon*: these are two chapels which were often built into the choir in Byzantine architecture. In front, opposite the apse and in a strangely oblique position in one of the angles of the perimeter, is the narthex, the old entrance to the church, an elongated porch contained on its short sides by two *esedrae* placed opposite each other. The different elements blend perfectly and the central part of the building is emphasized by a wonderful mixture of geometric shapes which all rotate around the central axis.

If from the outside the church of San Vitale gives an impression of rhythm and self-contained perfection, on the inside the effect of its circular harmony and lovely, shimmering mosaics depends upon the subtle play of light and shade. Thus the spectator's eye is drawn slowly, as if entranced, from the warm shadow of the double ambulatory to the clear light of the central space, and finally to the resplendent mosaics of the choir and apse. The mosaics were executed between 525 and 548, starting with the theophany of the apse, which we know was completed in the time of Bishop Ecclesius. The work continued with the scenes from the Old Testament in the choir, and finally, when the Byzantines were in control of the city and Maximian was the Archbishop of Ravenna, the two mosaics which depict the courts of Justinian and Theodora were completed. Most critics are now agreed that there are two basic styles apparent in the work of the artists who over a period of about twenty-five years took their turns on the scaffolding in the apse and the choir. The mosaics in the choir, lively and imaginative, are in the Hellenistic-Roman tradition, whereas the decoration of the apse is more formal and stylized.

The most important features of the choir are the two lunettes above the triforia of the lower part: these depict sacrifices which take place in the Old Testament, anticipations of the sacrifice of Christ Himself and the Eucharist. On the right are the Sacrifices of Abel and Melchizedek and on the left the Sacrifice of Isaac. The pictures of Moses, Jeremiah and Isaiah, the representatives of the twelve tribes of Israel, and the scenes showing Moses guarding his father-in-law's flock and preparing to approach the burning bush, complete, in perfect accordance, this part of the decoration. Above each lunette is a pair of angels, similar to the winged victories of ancient art, holding a medallion with a cross. These separate the lower part from the upper part, which in turn depicts characters and symbols from the New Testament. At the sides of the beautiful upper mullioned windows tower the powerful figures of the four Evangelists, recording the words of the Holy Spirit. Above them, the higher the mosaic decoration goes, the more abstract it becomes. Upward from the special symbols of the Evangelists (angel for Mathew, lion for Mark, bull for Luke, and eagle for John) the mosaics show only more symbols, decorative motifs, and celestial figures. The vine, the symbol of the body of the Church, spreads over the curved wall above the windows, while the cross-ribbed vault is covered with a magnificent and colorful array of fruit and flowers. In the middle of the ceiling four winged angels hold the wreath which surrounds the Lamb of God. This is not only the physical center of the decorated space but, symbolically, the key to the whole decoration.

On the intrados of the arch which forms the entrance to the choir the figures of Christ, the Twelve Apostles, St. Gervasius, and St. Protasius are depicted in fifteen medallions, while on the triumphal arch which leads into the apse, on either side of two angels holding a radial disc, the cities of Jerusalem and Bethlehem are shown against a gold background; symbolically these represent the whole human race (Jerusalem standing for the Jews and Bethlehem the Gentiles), redeemed and joining together in the sign of Christ. The mosaics in the choir were probably completed around the middle of the sixth century in the time of Bishop Ursicinius and Bishop Vittorius, and, as we have noted, they have a remarkable naturalistic quality. There is, in general, no stiffness in the figures. Their facial expressions and the positions in which they are placed are extraordinarily varied. The colors are rich and subtle; the perspective is well-planned and sound, and the landscape is an integral part of the whole decoration. In Abraham Sacrificing Isaac, for example, the Biblical scene is put into a totally naturalistc context: through the branches of the tree we can see purple clouds slipping by; there are rocks in the background, while the face of Abraham himself, as he is about to slay his son, reveals all the anguish inherent in the terrible deed. In the same way the four Evangelists are placed against a sloping background, the perspective of which is extremely carefully drawn. The scenes are rich in plants, birds and colors, while the figures which symbolize each Evangelist are astonishingly true to life. The lion is particularly noteworthy: tawny and snarling, this is a wonderful portrayal of pure animal ferocity. Wherever the artists who worked on the choir came from, these mosaics show that they were greatly influenced by the naturalism of ancient art. The weight of a tradition which went back nearly a thousand years to a large extent still governed their style.

If we move into the apse from the choir and look up at the solemn mosaic of the theophany, we are in a different world. Although the technique and colors are still in the Hellenistic-Roman tradition, and the naturalism is still there, the nature of the spiritual concept behind the arrangement of the figures shows a profound change. As Pietro Toesca says, "the sacred scene extends beyond reality and draws its inspiration from certain fixed ideas which were to endure in mediaeval art". The outstanding feature of this portrayal of Divine manifestation is a static, abstract quality, and the gesture with which the Christ offers the crown to San Vitale, while an angel introduces Bishop Ecclesius offering a model of the church, is regal and liturgical, no longer of this world. The unknown, possibly Byzantine, artist achieved the effect of a spiritual vision principally through the use of an abstract gold background, a disregard for perspective, and the totally frontal impact of the figures.

The same elements are present in the two decorations on the wall of the apse. On the left is Justinian's court, and on the right Theodora's. These were certainly executed in 548, when the church was consecrated, by artists in the pay of the Emperor. The Basileus, dressed in purple and gold with a crown resting on his head and a halo surrounding it, gives much the same impression as the figure of Christ in the dome of the apse. On the Emperor's right are two court officials and the praetorian guards — the symbols of his power on earth — while on his left we see his spiritual power symbolized by the figures of Archbishop Maximian and the priests. Justinian dominates the scene and expresses both aspects of a power which comes from God and which in some way connects him with the Almighty Himself. The Roman tradition of imperial rule has now changed completely into the theocratic order of the Byzantine rulers and, in so far as this sums up the Eastern concept of power, we might even say that the panel is a *manifesto politico*. Opposite this scene, in one equally solemn and formal, is shown the Empress Theodora with her court. Dressed in purple and weighed down with gold and jewels like some goddess, she is the eternal symbol of splendor and luxury. The daughter of the bear-trainer Acacius, who in her youth had been an actress and courtesan before Justinian fell in love with her and made her his Empress, is not seen in this decoration as the beautiful woman who played a part in one of the most romantic and famous stories in history. Instead, we see the idea of power embodied in her — a power which she is destined to wield until her death.

The colorful splendor of these two mosaics is no longer bent towards achieving a naturalistic effect, but something totally different: here physical characteristics are all but ignored, and the figures are shown as purely abstract beings, linked together in an almost ritualistic rhythm. However, there is still a trace of naturalism in one or two of the portraits. According to Giuseppe Bovini, the figure of Justinian himself was undoubtedly modelled on one of the many portraits of the Emperor which were sent out to the provinces, because it so closely resembles the description which Procopius of Caesarea gave of him: " ...in height he was neither greatly tall, nor small, but medium; nor was he thin but rather somewhat plump; his face, though greatly round, was not ugly

in color... I could not sum up his charac-
ter with perfect exactitude, for he was
by nature unpleasant and a simpleton, and,
in truth, a foolish knave..." (Procopius di
Caesarea: Historia arcana, VIII.)

San Vitale
Left wall of apse
and presbytery

SAN GIOVANNI EVANGELISTA

This church is one of the oldest and most famous in Ravenna. It is even older than San Vitale, for it was begun in 425 by Galla Placidia, who had it decorated with portraits of the family of Theodosius. Unfortunately fate has been particularly unkind to this building. A large number of restorations through the centuries have altered its appearance. The extensive cycle of mosaics which at one time decorated the interior has now been completely lost, and to cap it all the church was badly damaged in the last war. Today, after the recent restorations which have taken place, we can once more admire its simplicity and nobility. The interior is particularly striking. It is divided into three aisles by a series of slender columns, and the apse is enlivened by a row of round-arched windows which add to the brightness of the surroundings. The structure is so far simplified that if it were not for the clearly Oriental dosserets (the triangular elevation between the capital and the arch, typical of Byzantine architecture) we could almost imagine ourselves in some Early Christian basilica in Rome, of the type of Santa Sabina. From the outside it is the apse — of the polygonal form typical of Eastern architecture — which has preserved its original appearance more than any other part: it is still flanked by the *diaconicon* and *prothesis*.

San Giovanni
Evangelista
Interior

This is also known as the "Neonian Baptistery" because, as the ancient historian Andrea-Agnello, in his "Liber Pontificalis" states, around or shortly after the middle of the fifth century, Bishop Neon arranged for the decoration of the interior. However, the building itself is almost fifty years older, and must have been built in the time of Bishop Ursus, along with the Cathedral of which it forms an integral part. In the seventh century certain alterations were made to the upper part.

From the outside the building is octagonal in shape and, as is common in so many of Ravenna's monuments, there is a marked contrast between the plain exterior and the rich decoration inside. The mosaic over the rounded arches which encircle the lower zone, with its spirals of acanthus sparkling with gold against a blue background, has a great deal in common with that of the Mausoleum of Galla Placidia, in both subject-matter and execution. Despite the fact that a large part was restored in the nineteenth century, this thick foliage is really beautiful as it curls slowly over the wall, surrounding male figures clothed in white, and it fits in perfectly with the rest of the decoration. The upper zone with the windows, which forms the drum of the cupola, gives the illusion of being a gallery; it is decorated with stucco reliefs which at one time must have been brightly colored. These stuccos, which portray male figures (possibly Old Testament prophets) placed inside niches of various shapes, have great elegance, and the skill with which they are executed indicates that the classical tradition was still very much alive.

The same factors are evident in the mosaics which cover the inside of the cupola in three concentric circles. In the center the unknown artists who decorated the Baptistery have depicted the Baptism of Christ. Unfortunately, as Bovini points out, a large section of the central part of the scene, including the head and arm of John the Baptist, the face of Christ, and the Dove symbolizing the Holy Spirit, was entirely restored in the nineteenth century. Enough of the original remains intact, however, to show its vivid naturalism and the strong influence of ancient art. This is revealed in the flowers, plants and grass on the banks of the Jordan, in the figure of the bearded old man rising from the water, who personifies the river itself, and in the precise physical differences which distinguish Christ and the Baptist.

In a circle around the Baptism, set against a deep blue background and separated from each other by gilded acanthus plants, are the figures of the Twelve Apostles. Dressed in cloaks alternately white and gold, each carrying a crown in his hand, symbol of heavenly glory, the Apostles move along briskly, almost gaily, and seem fully aware of their humanity and individuality. One senses real bodies under the cloaks. Each face is both physically and psychologically different from any other. As we can see from a comparison with the mosaics in the apse of San Vitale, or better still, with the processions of Martyrs and Virgins in Sant'Apollinare Nuovo, this style is vastly different from the impersonality of Byzantine art. If it is possible, in view of the exceptional quality and intensity of the colors, to make any comparison, the most suitable (as W. F. Volbach suggests) is with the splen-

did Early Christian mosaics of Hosios David at Thessalonica.

In the circle below the Apostles the decorative pattern is of so obscure a nature that it has given rise to widely differing interpretations. The elements which recur again and again are an altar with an open book, and an empty throne surmounted by a cross. The open book probably symbolizes the sanctity of the Gospels, and the empty throne with the cross suggests the presence of an invisible God. Some interpret the whole as a picture of the heavenly city with the empty seats awaiting the chosen ones; others interpret the seats and altars as part of the background of the Apostles, but placed below them, without reference to their position in perspective. Whatever the full meaning behind the pattern may be, there is no doubt as to the realism of the treatment and the artist's feeling for color and elegance of form. This work has its roots firmly planted in the Hellenistic-Roman tradition.

Baptistery
of the Cathedral
Exterior

BAPTISTERY OF THE ARIANS

This building is called the Arian Baptistery in order to distinguish it from the older Neonian Baptistery; it was probably built in the time of Theodoric, towards the end of the fifth century, when Arianism was the official religion of the court and the barbarian elite in power, while the Latin population remained Catholic. In fact, apart from theological differences concerning the nature of Christ, when it came to the organization of the church and the liturgy these two forms of Christianity had a great deal in common. This is plain from the fact that the Arian Baptistery is not only architecturally similar to the Neonian Baptistery, but also portrays the same scenes in its mosaics.

As in the Neonian Baptistery, the central space of the cupola depicts the Baptism of Christ. Here Christ is shown as a beardless, naked youth, half-submerged in the waters of the Jordan, while above him John the Baptist, wearing a leopard skin, stretches out his right hand and gives the blessing. On the left is a white-haired old man in a green cloak: he is the classical personification of the river. Apart from a few variations, this scene is exactly the same as the Baptism scene in the Neonian Baptistery. Again, in a circle around the central medallion is the procession of Apostles, robed in white and carryng the triumphal crown in their partially covered hands. They all share the same heavenly glory, which is symbolized by the rich gold background. The complex ring of symbolic images which made up the outer band in the Neonian Baptistery does not vanish altogether but is reduced to a single element, the empty throne with the cross, which is here placed between St. Peter and St. Paul. Much more obvious than the iconographical differences are the differences of style. Although Theodoric's mosaicists took practically all their inspiration from the artists before them who worked on the Neonian Baptistery, they seem more wooden than the latter, less sensitive to the color and naturalism of the old tradition. The unvarying gold background becomes too predominant. The Apostles no longer have the look of individual portraits; the colors are flat and cold, and the decorative details much less intricate and subtle.

Baptistery
of the Arians
Exterior

We know for certain, from Andrea-Agnello's "Liber Pontificalis", that this church was built, probably at the beginning of the sixth century, by Theodoric, and that he dedicated it to Christ the Redeemer. Originally it was an Arian church, but ceased to be when the power of the Goths ended and the Byzantines took control of the city. At this time unorthodoxy was suppressed and all Arian churches were promptly handed over to the Catholics; the Arian Baptistery became Santa Maria in Cosmedin, and Theodoric's Basilica of the Redeemer was dedicated to St. Martin of Tours. There was nothing casual in naming it after St. Martin for, as Bovini points out, this man was famous for his lifelong struggle against heresy, and to rename perhaps the best known center of Arianism after him was a proud affirmation of victory on the part of Ravenna's Catholics. The church was only given its present name around the middle of the ninth century, when the remains of St. Apollinaris were transfered there from the Basilica of Classe which, because of its vulnerable position, was at that time threatened by the frequent raids of Adriatic pirates.

Next to the building is a round bell tower, characteristic of Ravenna's churches. The marble portico in front of the church was built in the sixteenth century. The interior, with its three aisles, has also undergone extensive alterations through the centuries. The most important of these took place in the sixteenth century, when the columns of the central nave were raised, and this destroyed the two strips of brick, probably inlaid with marble, which separated the arches from the mosaics. The present close proximity of the figures to the columns, which could not have been foreseen by the architect, somewhat alters the proportions of the interior. Finally, the apse, which was destroyed by an earthquake in the eighth century and again damaged in the last war, is also a reconstruction.

Both walls of the central nave are covered with mosaics, divided into three horizontal zones, which for their size and quality and remarkably good condition are among the finest examples of Ravenna's art. These mosaics are also important because in them are seen two different periods and styles, some fifty years apart. The two upper rows, which show scenes from the life of Christ and the Prophets, were executed earlier, in the time of Theodoric, while the figures of the Virgins and the Martyrs were done on the order of Bishop Agnello shortly after the middle of the sixth century, when the Arian church had just passed into the hands of the Catholics.

The scenes from the life of Christ on the upper band of both walls are arranged in two sequences: on the left wall Christ's miracles are depicted, and on the right wall scenes from the Passion. It may seem strange to us that instead of being the central part of the decoration, the scenes from the life of Christ are placed just below the ceiling, and this would certainly have been unthinkable during the Romanesque and Gothic periods; but there was nothing odd about this in an age in which symbolic figures were so important that anything which was narrative, as opposed to expressing an ideal, was placed in a less conspicuous position. Besides, the scenes from the life of Christ are not a complete retelling of the Gospel, but only depict the parts of the Bible which were read in Ravenna during Lent. Although these two series of Biblical scenes are both typical of the time of Theodoric, we can detect two different hands at work in them, for the Passion scenes show certain differences in style from the Miracle scenes. The style of the artist who executed the latter seems stiffer, his color and technique less refined, and his scenes are notably less crowded than the Passion scenes. The artist who worked on the Passion scenes shows a remarkable feeling for expression and color, and is more inclined to naturalism. These scenes, almost always dramatic and emotional, are on a generally higher level. Both artists seem to have been inspired by contemporary illuminated manuscripts from Constantinople, although their Western taste makes them emphasize intensity of line and contrast of light and shade.

Immediately below the Gospel scenes thirty-two prophets clothed in white stand out against a gold background, separated from each other by the small arched windows. Notwithstanding their static, rigidly frontal attitudes, and the way their gestures are repeated, the figures maintain a certain individuality, and there is a sense of solidity in the modelling. This is clear evidence that the work was executed in the time of Theodoric, when the Hellenistic-Roman tradition, even though on the wane, was still a strong influence. It is in any case not improbable that, as A. Grabar suggests, these figures derive from the series of statues of dignitaries which, placed in niches, often adorned secular buildings in the East.

The two famous processions of Martyrs and Virgins, on the other hand, date from the time of Bishop Agnellus. The Martyrs are preceded by St. Martin and approach the figure of Christ, while the Virgins are led by the Three Wise Men and move towards the Madonna and Child. These mosaics are so different from the others, both visually and in the basic idea which lies behind them, that we can now call this style Byzantine. There is barely any trace of individuality in the figures as they glide slowly against the gold background, their gestures and their facial expressions all alike. They are linked in a kind of secret rhythm which is perceptible only if one looks at the Procession as a whole. The human body is now no more than a symbol, a white or gilded chrysalis, representing an unutterable, incomprehensible state of being far removed from this world. The sumptuous garments cover forms that have no semblance of solidity, and in the reiteration of the gestures, the mechanically identical expressions, there is such a deliberate departure from reality that it can only be explained as a different way of seeing things. These artists worked almost entirely in terms of concepts and ideals. In short, with these mosaics, which in Bovini's excellent phrase are "pictorial litanies", we leave the Late Classical world to enter the sphere of abstract and esoteric art known as Byzantine.

Finally, let us examine the two beautiful panels at the beginning of the right and left walls. On the right is Theodoric's palace, and on the left the port of Classis. These mosaics, executed during Theodoric's reign, give us a precise idea of pre-Byzantine architecture in Ravenna and are a great help in imagining what his great capital looked like. In them we can still

see traces of the robes worn by personages
at the court of the Gothic king, a part
of the decoration which was destroyed on
the orders of Bishop Agnellus.

Sant'Apollinare
Nuovo
Madonna and
Child with Angels

This is a small, simple church. The plain brick façade is enlivened by a small mullioned window in the center, and it is interesting to note how the large square bell tower is lightened by the effect of the mullioned windows placed above each other on each of the four sides, which grow from two to three to four mullions as the tower rises. The interior is divided into three aisles, there is a trussed ceiling, and the semicircular apse at the far end is pierced by a row of windows half way up, thus repeating the neat and striking plan of San Giovanni Evangelista.

In point of fact, as recent studies have proved beyond doubt, the church of San Francesco as it exists today is the result of a series of alterations, most of which took place between the eighth and tenth centuries; therefore its basic structure reveals the somewhat advanced and involuted stage which architecture had reached in Ravenna at this time. The original *Apostoleion* (the church dedicated to the Apostles), which stood on the site of the present church, must have been very different. Andrea-Agnello mentions the mosaics which Bishop Neon ordered around the middle of the fifth century, but which no longer exist. The only works of art which could conceivably date from the time of Bishop Neon, and may be even earlier, are the several ancient sarcophagi inside the church. The most notable of these, possibly dating from the fourth century, is one which shows the figures of Christ and the Apostles and now forms the front part of the high altar.

However, San Francesco is less noted for its architectural details and its sculpture than for having been linked for centuries with the memory of Dante Alighieri. As is common knowledge, this great Florentine died in exile in Ravenna in 1321, and it was in this church that his first funeral rites were performed. For many years his body lay in an ancient marble sarcophagus in the grounds of the church. It was then moved several times before being finally laid to rest a short distance away from the church in a Neoclassical temple erected in 1780 by the Ravenna architect Camillo Morigia. Inside the small chapel, still the goal of endless numbers of pilgrims, is an idealized portrait of the poet in bas-relief which was carved in marble in 1483 by the Venetian Pietro Lombardo.

SANT'APOLLINARE IN CLASSE

One of the main reasons for the fasci nation this great church — one of the most famous of all Christian churches — holds for visitors is its isolated position. It stands a long way from the center of the city in the midst of a wide expanse of countryside, where the tang of the Adriatic is in the air. However, the church has not always enjoyed this romantic isolation. When, in 549, Archbishop Maximian consecrated the imposing edifice which had been built with Giuliano Argentario's wealth, and dedicated it to St. Apollinaris (the first bishop of Ravenna, and the man who had first brought the Gospel to this particular area), the church stood in the middle of the city of Classis with its famous port, rich in industry and trade. It was only later, as the coastline gradually receded and the sources of the port's prosperity dried up, that the area became virtually deserted. So Sant'Apollinare dates from the height of the city's Byzantine period, when the great Maximian was in charge of the archdiocese of Ravenna, and Byzantium was in firm control of Italy. In contrast, however, to San Vitale, with its central plan, probably inspired by the churches of the East although it also took a great deal from late Classical architecture, Sant'Apollinare is an expression of the new Christian and Western adaptation of the basilican form.

Indeed, except for a four-sided portico which no longer exists, and excluding the round bell tower which was a later, possibly tenth-century addition, we can say that this church is one of the most perfect and best-preserved examples of the classic Christian basilica. Each of its architectural features stands out clearly — the narthex, which has on its left a rectang-

ular building, the central nave, raised one story above the side aisles, and the polygonal apse flanked by the *prothesis* and *diaconicon*. The exterior of the building, as was common in Ravenna, is of plain brick; its neat simplicity would seem a good indication of what lies inside. But as soon as one passes the threshold of the church the sumptuousness of the interior stands out in strong contrast to the austere, modest appearance of the exterior. One has the feeling of being carried into another dimension, far removed from the physical world. The light that filters in through the windows of the aisles and apse, shimmering with color over the mosaics, makes the atmosphere seem alive; it makes one think of the spiritual splendor of the Kingdom of God, and of the "Civitas Dei" dreamed of by the Fathers of the Church. We must also remember that today the overall effect of the interior is much less impressive than it was before Sigismondo Malatesta, the Lord of Rimini, had the precious marble panels that formerly covered the side walls carried off, in the middle of the fifteenth century, to decorate the Temple that bears his name.

The heart of Sant'Apollinare in Classe, and the point to which one's attention is inevitably drawn, with its subtle light and soft, dreamlike colors, is the semidome of the apse, entirely covered, as is the triumphal arch which leads into it, with glittering mosaics. The upper part of the arch is dominated by the figure of Christ, flanked by the symbols of the four Evangelists, set against a deep blue sky streaked with clouds. The frowning face of the Christ is set in an expression that shows a somber and pessimistic conception of

Francesco
tro Lombardo:
nb of Dante

the Savior which, together with a certain stiffness in the style, would suggest that this mosaic, and the others on the upper part of the arch, were executed, as Pietro Toesca has indicated, in the seventh century. The decoration of this part of the triumphal arch is completed by the symbolic representations of the cities of Jerusalem and Bethlehem, from which two lines of white lambs emerge. The idea of this scene, one commonly used in the first centuries after Christ, is that of the double church of the Jews and Gentiles, setting out towards the judgment of Christ. The two palm trees set against a deep blue background and the figures of the archangels Michael and Gabriel on the sides of the arch date from the sixth century. However, the mosaics showing St. Matthew and St. Luke are much later and were possibly executed in the twelfth century.

The mosaics in the apse, which date from the middle of the sixth century, portray, in Toesca's phrase, "one of the most extraordinary allegorical ideas ever conceived in art". The refinement of the figures, the abstract forms and colors, and the extremely intellectualized nature of the subject matter produce a poetic effect of a quality unparalleled in the history of Western art. Set against a rich, green valley, with the trees, birds and flowers giving a dreamlike picture of the gardens of heaven, stands the figure of St. Apollinaris, Bishop of Ravenna. Around him, spread along the bottom curve of the semidome, are twelve lambs. These represent the Christian people, entrusted by God to the care of His shepherd and led by Him to the Everlasting Life. Above this, the unknown artist of Sant'Apollinare

has depicted in an even more abstract way the Biblical scene of the Transfiguration on the Mount. Between the figures of Elijah and Moses, and in the center of a great medallion, shines a large cross, symbol of the Transfigured Christ. The three white lambs represent the three Apostles who according to the Gospel witnessed the miracle. Below the semidome of the apse, in the spaces between the windows, each under a shell-shaped canopy, stand the figures of the Bishops Severus, Ecclesius, Ursus, and Ursicinius, wearing their sacred vestments. They represent the historical continuity of the Church in Ravenna. Founded by St. Apollinaris, its orthodoxy was defended and its power strengthened and increased by these bishops, the legitimate successors of the Saint. The faces of the bishops are individual portraits; this is the only part of the decoration of Sant'Apollinare where any trace of Occidental realism can still be noted.

In the apse-mosaics of Sant'Apollinare in Classe sixth-century Byzantine art unquestionably reached its zenith. It would be difficult indeed to advance beyond this precarious point where a profound intellectualism and a high order of artistic expression fuse and maintain a miraculous balance. Thus it is hardly surprising that after this climax the quality of pictorial art in Ravenna slowly declined. We can see this from the two mosaic panels, possibly dating from the seventh century, on the side walls of the apse. On the right are shown the sacrifices of Abel, Abraham, and Melchizedek and on the left we see the Emperor Constantine IV Pogonatus in the act of granting the privileges to the ambassador of Archbishop Maurus.

Even if it is difficult to criticise the latter scene fairly, since it has been heavily restored in recent times, the two mosaics, besides taking all their ideas from the famous imperial portraits in the apse of San Vitale, display a marked poverty of expression. The colors are weak, and the scenes show signs of haste and are less skilfully worked out.

Sant'Apollinare
in Classe
Donation
of Constantine
(detail)

THEODORIC'S PALACE
AND MAUSOLEUM

As menacing and mysterious as some monstrous object flung from a distant planet, the tomb of the barbarian king stands isolated on the outskirts of Ravenna. Facing its great bulk one has the feeling that one is looking at an enormous piece of flotsam cast up after some historic shipwreck. It is not difficult to see why since ancient times strange and somber legends have been woven around this building, for even today it is difficult to approach the imposing mass without experiencing a vague feeling of awe.

The tomb of Theodoric, who died in 526, was built with great blocks of Istrian stone. It has a central plan and consists of two ten-sided sections, one inside the other. Encircling the base, a series of deep rounded niches recall in their shape and proportions the architectural rhythms of Roman monuments. On each of the sides of the upper part there is a shallow recess in the shape of a blind mullioned window. At one time there was probably a covered gallery, supported by slender columns, which went round the upper part of the building, where we now see an iron railing.

The most striking and original feature of the building, however, is the roof. Circular in shape, hewn from a single huge piece of Istrian stone, it is about thirty-six feet in diameter and weighs around three hundred tons. Around its rim are twelve pierced buttresses. Seen from below the roof of Theodoric's Mausoleum makes one think, as has been remarked, of the helmet of a fantastic warrior. It gives an impression of sullen strength, of a savage violence truly barbarian. On the other hand this roof is so strange and unique that one scholar has

put forward the theory that it is in fact an imitation in stone of the circular shape of a barbarian tent. If this is the case, the twelve buttresses around the rim of the dome would refer to the poles that support the roof of the tent and whose ends jut out, while the curious "claw" motif which appears in the frieze just below them, totally unknown in Western art, would then refer to metal hooks, part of a device — still used by certain nomadic tribes today — for sliding back the flaps of the tent. It is after all quite possible that the barbarian king would have wanted his burial place to remind his wandering people of the way they had lived for centuries. If we accept this hypothesis there is clearly a romantic aspect to this remarkable monument, witness to the domination of Italy by the Goths. It is, however, necessary to state that this "Germanic" interpretation of the tomb of Theodoric is in considerable contrast with what is historically known of the king's personality; for all his life he was profoundly under the influence of Latin culture and civilization. And besides, the technical details of the construction (the expert fitting together of the stones, the complicated vaulting of the lower chamber, etc.) show such complete mastery of classical building methods that the architect must certainly have been trained within the Roman-Oriental tradition. Perhaps the key to the understanding of this unique monument is to be sought — as has been suggested — in ancient Syrian art.

Today the Mausoleum of Theodoric is merely an empty shell; the bones of the king were probably removed and scattered when the city fell under the power of Byzantium and orthodox Catholicism asserted itself with all its intolerance. Thus it is difficult to know whether the sarcophagus was in the cruciform space in the lower part or, as is more likely, in the upper part, where there is still a basin made of porphyry, presumably intended for funerary purposes.

In contrast to the Mausoleum, the so-called Palace of Theodoric has no connection whatsoever with the Arian king, and indeed, as practically all scholars agree, it does not even belong to the sixth century, but to a considerably later era. It is obvious that this building could not have been Theodoric's palace, not only on stylistic grounds but also because we know what his real palace looked like from the mosaic in Sant'Apollinare Nuovo, and

the excavations and surveys which took place at the beginning of this century proved beyond any shadow of doubt that his real palace stood next to the Arian basilica. But we have still not discovered the original purpose of this building. Today little remains of it except the brick façade, which is enlivened by a central doorway below a large niche and by lateral porticoes with blind arches above. Scholars have made various and contradictory suggestions concerning the function of the building: the narthex of a church, a guard house, the offices of the exarch's secretaries. However, they are all agreed that is was built fairly late, between the seventh and eighth centuries.

Mausoleum
of Theodoric
Aerial view

We owe the beginnings of the museum to the learned monks of Classe, who even at the beginning of the eighteenth century showed an interest in mediaeval art unusual in those times. They collected and classified works of various periods from many different places of origin. When, after the Napoleonic invasion, the religious orders were suppressed, the collection passed first into the care of the municipal government and then, after some lucky discoveries and important additions had been made, into the hands of the State. Just before the outbreak of World War I it was moved to its present site, an ex-Benedictine monastery next to the church of San Vitale. Today the museum is divided into various departments, and as a whole gives an extremely good idea of Ravenna's art through the centuries. The collections in the first and second cloisters are particularly important. Most of the space is taken up with sculpture dating from the Classical, Early Christian, and Byzantine periods, but here we need only mention the marble remains of the Porta Aurea which the Emperor Claudius built in 43 A. D.; the famous relief dating from the first century which depicts the deification of Augustus; the large number of *stelae*, funeral pillars of the Roman era, of which the most outstanding is the one made for

Publius Longidienus, a naval carpenter of Classis who had himself depicted, with great realism, engaged in his daily work; and the renowned sarcophagus of the *Traditio Legis.* The upper rooms contain the museum's many separate collections, including coins, weapons, ceramics, small bronzes, and the fascinating collection of Creto-Venetian icons. Room IX, with its collection of antique textiles, and Room X, with its ivories, are of particular importance. In Room IX, the silk material which comes from the tomb of San Giuliano in Rimini is especially noteworthy. It is a very rare piece, probably dating from the ninth century, and shows how much the Byzantine textile-makers depended on the decorative motifs of Sassanid-Persian art. In Room X two pieces in particular stand out for their antiquity and perfect craftsmanship. These are the tablet depicting the Apollo and Daphne of pagan mythology, which was made in some Egyptian workshop in the fifth century, and the so-called Diptych of Murano, the latter a cover for the Gospels decorated with the figure of Christ in triumph among saints and various scenes from the Old and New Testaments. In this piece are still found all the liveliness of expression and technical skill of Hellenistic ivory carving.

CHAPEL AND MUSEUM OF
THE ARCHBISHOP

The Archbishop's Museum in Ravenna is worth a visit, if only to see the famous throne of Maximian, a relic which in Bovini's phrase is "the most beautiful work in ivory which the ancient world has handed down to us". The throne was originally a gift from Justinian to Bishop Maximian (whose monogram can be seen on the upper frieze), before he became Archbishop, as a token of gratitude towards the man who more than any other had worked for the success of the Byzantine cause in Italy. It is safe to say that it was made in the first half of the sixth century, in some famous workshop of the East which dealt with orders from the Court and specialized in pieces of great value and exceptionally fine quality. At least four master artists worked on the throne, and it is to the

Chapel of the
Archbishop's Palace
St. Perpetua

credit of modern scholarship that their individual styles have been recognised. The front of the seat, showing the figures of John the Baptist and the four Evangelists, is the work of an Eastern craftsman, possibly from Constantinople. A refinement bordering on the effete, a noble melancholy, marks these five saints, in whose faces there seems to shine the lofty, detached idealism of the ancient philosophers.

The artist who executed the decorative friezes framing these panels shows greater liveliness and imagination than the first master, and great feeling for pictorial effects and those of light and shade. The recurring motif is the undulating vine whose wide curves shelter a lively assortment of birds and beasts, caught in the most varied poses. A supremely sure hand has been at work here, bringing out the most delicate effects of light and shade, revealing the bloom of ripe fruit, the lion about to spring, the alert caution of the stag, the ram's thick fleece, the plumage of the peacock. In the short space of a few strips of ivory the unknown, possibly Syrian, artist, gives us a fascinating exhibition of his technical skill and feeling for naturalism. The quality of the work falls off to some degree in the panels on the back of the throne, which are the work of a third artist, while it reaches perhaps its highest point in the side panels, where episodes from the life of Joseph of the Old Testament are depicted. This, the work of a fourth master, possibly from Alexandria, is remarkable for its narrative flow, the incisiveness of the carving, and the liveliness of the pictorial effects.

There are many other things of great

historical and artistic interest in the museum — the large, headless porphyry statue, probably a portrait of the Emperor Justinian, to mention only one.

The main attraction of the Archbishop's palace, apart from Maximian's throne, is the small chapel, decorated with mosaics, which was built by Bishop Petrus II between the fifth and sixth centuries. Unfortunately, the mosaics have been altered so much through the centuries that today most of them can only be regarded as restorations and reworkings dating from different periods. The best preserved parts are the decorations on the vault of the vestibule, with a sophisticated motif of white lilies and birds of many colors, and on the vault of the chapel itself, where four angels robed in white, with the symbols of the four Evangelists between them, hold up a disc bearing Christ's initials in Greek. The style of these mosaics in the Archibishop's chapel is typical of the time of Theodoric, notably realistic, still to a certain extent in the Hellenistic-Roman tradition.

Archiepiscpal
Museum
Headless statue

This gallery, formerly situated in the Academy of Fine Arts and now in the Loggia del Giardino, contains for the most part local paintings of the fifteenth and sixteenth centuries. These give us a good idea of the modest but by no means negligible artistic movements which took place in Ravenna during the Renaissance. The most important painters in Ravenna during this period were Niccolò Rondinelli and Francesco Zaganelli da Cotignola, both of whom are well represented in the gallery. Rondinelli was a close follower of Bellini; his calm, modest paintings openly owe their inspiration to the work of his great master. Zaganelli, livelier by temperament, and more eclectic, was influenced by the Ferrarese school of the late fifteenth century, by the Bolognese artist Aspertini, the engravings of Albrecht Dürer, and by the Venetian painters of his own day. Of a later generation, and a painter decidedly inferior to these, is the local mannerist Luca Lon-

ghi, whose work is a tired echo of Florentine and Roman figure-painting.

The other works in the Academy are of the Venetian school (to which Antonio Vivarini's "Crucifixion" belongs), the school of Romagna, represented here by Baldassare Carrari and Marco Palmezzano, who both came from Forlì, and the Emilian school, which embraces such painters as Ludovico Carracci, Guercino, and Tiarini. Most of these pictures come from the monasteries and churches of Ravenna. One of the most popular sculptures of the Italian Renaissance is also in this gallery — the statue of Guidarello Guidarelli, which was carved around 1531 by the Venetian Tullio Lombardo. The young warrior, dressed completely ready for battle, lies on the marble slab, looking as if he were asleep. His beautiful young face is endowed with such intense pathos and conscious idealism that the statue fully deserves the romantic aura which has grown up around it.

ESSENTIAL BIBLIOGRAPHY

C. Ricci, *Guida di Ravenna* - Bologna, 1923.

P. Toesca, *Storia dell'arte italiana, vol. I "Il Medioevo"*, Turin, 1927.

P. Toesca, *S. Vitale di Ravenna. I Mosaici* - Milan, 1952.

W. F. Volbach, M. Hirmer, *Frühchristliche Kunst* - Munich, 1958.

G. Bovini, *Chiese di Ravenna* - Novara, 1957.

A. Grabar, *L'âge d'or de Justinien* - Paris, 1966.

G. Bovini, *Ravenna città d'arte* - Ravenna, 1968.

For detailed information on the bibliography of ancient Ravenna and its monuments cf. G. Bovini, *Principale bibliografia su Ravenna antica e sui suoi più importanti* - Faenza, 1957.

Mausoleum
of Galla Placidia

Interior

The building and its mosaics date from the first half of the 5th Century

Mausoleum
of Galla Placidia
Stags at the Spring

Mausoleum
of Galla Placidia
St. Lawrence Goes
to his Martyrdom

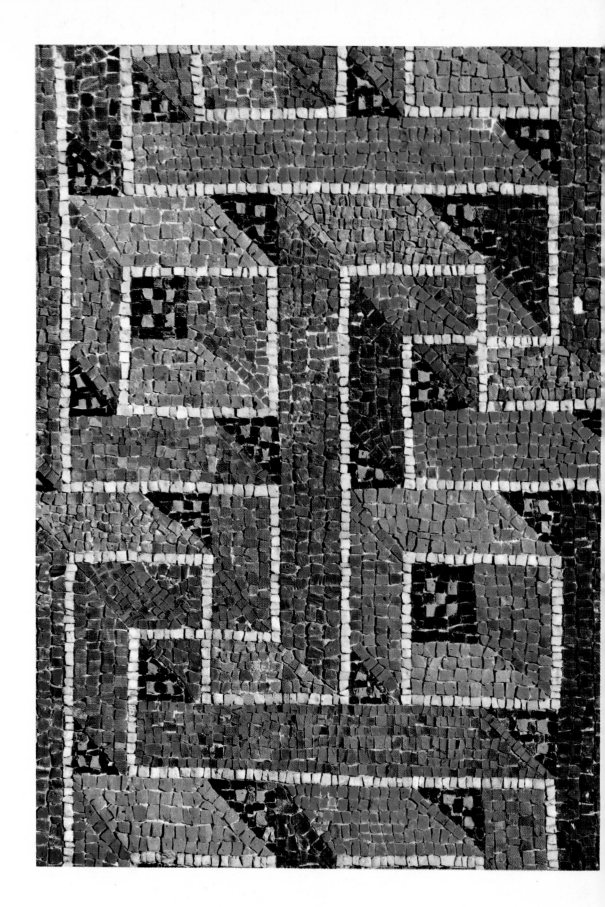

Mausoleum
of Galla Placidia
Decorative pattern

▲
Mausoleum
of Galla Placidia
The Doves at the
Fountain

▶
Mausoleum
of Galla Placidia
An Apostle

▶▶
Mausoleum
of Galla Placidia
Decorative pattern with
flowers and fruit

Mausoleum
of Galla Placidia
Lunette with
the Good Shepherd

Mausoleum
of Galla Placidia
Detail of the ceiling
covered with stars

San Vitale

Exterior

The church was built between 525 and 547 A.D.

Interior

San Vitale
The Bull
(symbol of St. Luke)

San Vitale
The Eagle
(symbol of St. John)

San Vitale
The Lion
(symbol of St. Mark)

▶
San Vitale
Abraham Entertains
Three Angels
(detail of the left
lunette)

San Vitale
The Apse

▶

San Vitale
St. Vitalis
(detail of apse)

▶▶

San Vitale
Ceiling of the choir
with the Lamb of God
amid four angels

42

◀
San Vitale
A Capital

▶
San Vitale
The Emperor Justinian

▶▶
San Vitale
The Court of Justinian
On the right is
Archbishop Maximian
with the clergy; on the
left are court officials
and the Praetorian
Guards.

◄
San Vitale
The Court of Theodora;
detail of courtier
holding a curtain

▶
San Vitale
The Empress Theodora

▶▶
San Vitale
The Court of the
Empress Theodora

Baptistery
of the Cathedral

Altar with open Book
(detail of the cupola)

◀

Interior

The building and
the mosaics date from
the first decades
of the 5th Century

▶

Mosaic decoration
of the cupola

Baptistery
of the Cathedral
Saint Peter
(detail of the cupola)

Baptistery of the Arians

Interior

Mosaics of the cupola.
The building dates
from the last years
of the 5th Century.

Baptistery
of the Arians
St. Paul
(detail of the cupola)

Baptistery
of the Arians
St. Peter
(detail of the cupola)

Sant'Apollinare Nuovo

Exterior

The church was built between the end of the 5th Century and the beginning of the 6th Century

Interior

Sant'Apollinare Nuovo
The Port of Classis
(detail of left wall)

Sant'Apollinare Nuovo
The Procession
of the Virgins
(left wall)

Sant'Apollinare Nuovo
The Three Wise Men
(detail of left wall)

4

1

5

2

6

3

7

 8

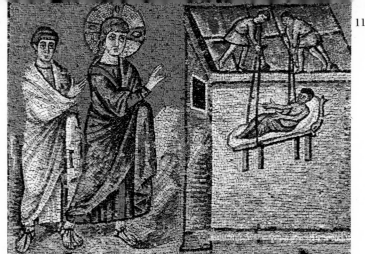 11

 9

 12

 10

 13

8 The Pharisee and the
   Publican at the Gate
   of the Temple

9 The Widow's Mite

10 Separation of the Sheep
   from the Goats

11 Healing of the Cripple
   of Capernaeum

12 Casting Out of
   the Devil

13 Healing of the Cripple
   of Bethesda

Sant'Apollinare Nuovo
Procession of the
Martyrs (right wall)

Sant'Apollinare Nuovo
The Palace (detail of
right wall)

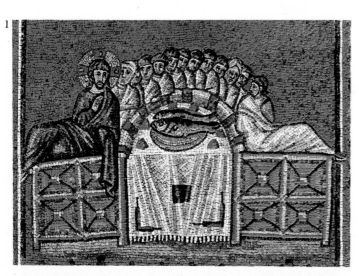

8 Judas Repentant

9 Christ Before Pilate

10 The Road to Calvary

11 The Two Marys at the
   Sepulchre

12 On the Road
   to Emmaus

13 The Unbelief
   of Thomas

Sant'Apollinare Nuovo
Dolphin (detail of the
Calling of Peter and
Andrew)

San Francesco

◀

Exterior

Originally built during
the 5th Century,
it was reconstructed
between the 9th and
the 11th Centuries

▼

Fifth century
sarcophagus with
Christ and the Apostles

Theodoric's Palace and Mausoleum

Exterior

The so-called Palace of Theodoric was built between the 7th and the 8th Centuries.

The Mausoleum
of Theodoric

Sant'Apollinare
in Classe

Exterior

The church was built
in the first half of
the 6th Century
and was consecrated
in 549 by Archbishop
Maximian

▶▶

The Apse

Interior

Sant'Apollinare
in Classe
The Cross of
St. Apollinaris
(detail of apse)

▶

Sant'Apollinare
in Classe
The Mystic
Meadow
(detail of apse)

Sant'Apollinare
in Classe
Christ Blessing
(detail of
triumphal arch)

Sant'Apollinare
in Classe
The Bishop Ursicinus
(detail of apse)

◀

Sant'Apollinare
in Classe
The Archangel Michaei
(detail of
triumphal arch)

▶

Sant'Apollinare
in Classe
The Symbol of
St. Luke the Evangelist
(detail of triumphal
arch)

Sant'Apollinare
in Classe
The Celestial City
of Bethlehem (detail
of triumphal arch)

Sant'Apollinare
in Classe
Sarcophagus of the
Twelve Apostles

National Museum

Roman funeral stele
to Publius Longidienus

National Museum
Ivory tablet with Apollo and Daphne;
Coptic art of the 5th Century

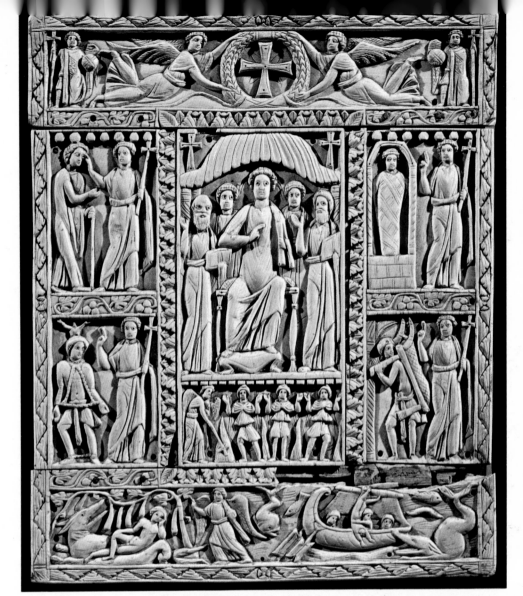

National Museum
The "Diptych
of Murano"; ivory,
5th to 6th Century

National Museum
Silk material from
the Orient, dating from
the 9th Century

Chapel and Museum
of the Archbishop

◄

Interior

The building and
the mosaics date from
the 5th and 6th
Centuries.

▶

Chapel of the
Archbishop
Detail of the ceiling
mosaics

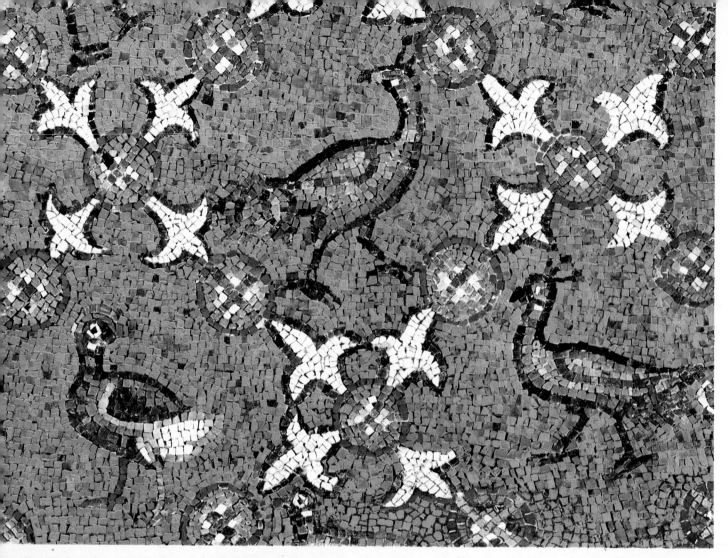

EGO VERI
SVM TAS ET
VIA VITA ✝

Chapel of the
Archbishop
◀
Detail of the ceiling
mosaics
◀◀
"The Greek Madonna"
◀
St. Paul

Chapel of the
Archbishop
Christ Militant

Archiepiscopal Museum
Scene from the Story
of Joseph
(panel from Archbishop
Maximian's Throne)

Archiepiscopal Museum
The Marriage in Cana
(panel from Archbishop
Maximian's Throne)

Archiepiscopal Museum
John the Baptist and
the Evangelists
(from Archbishop
Maximian's Throne)

Archiepiscopal
Museum
Throne of
Archbishop
Maximian

Cathedral

Exterior

The site now occupied by the Cathedral
was formerly that of the Basilica Ursiana,
one of the greatest and most famous
monuments of ancient Ravenna, built by
Archbishop Ursus at the beginning
of the 5th Century. The present mediocre
building is by the architect
G. Francesco Buonamici of Rimini, who in 1734
demolished the ancient basilica in order
to build the Cathedral.

▶

Chapel of the Sacrament
Guido Reni and pupils
Christ in Glory

Loggia del Giardino

Exterior
The very elegant
façade has two tiers
of fully rounded arches;
it is the work of
Lombard artists (1508).

▲
Niccolò Rondinelli:
The Virgin and Child
Enthroned with Saints

◄

Antonio Vivarini:
Crucifixion

▲

Francesco Zaganelli:
Crucifixion and Saints

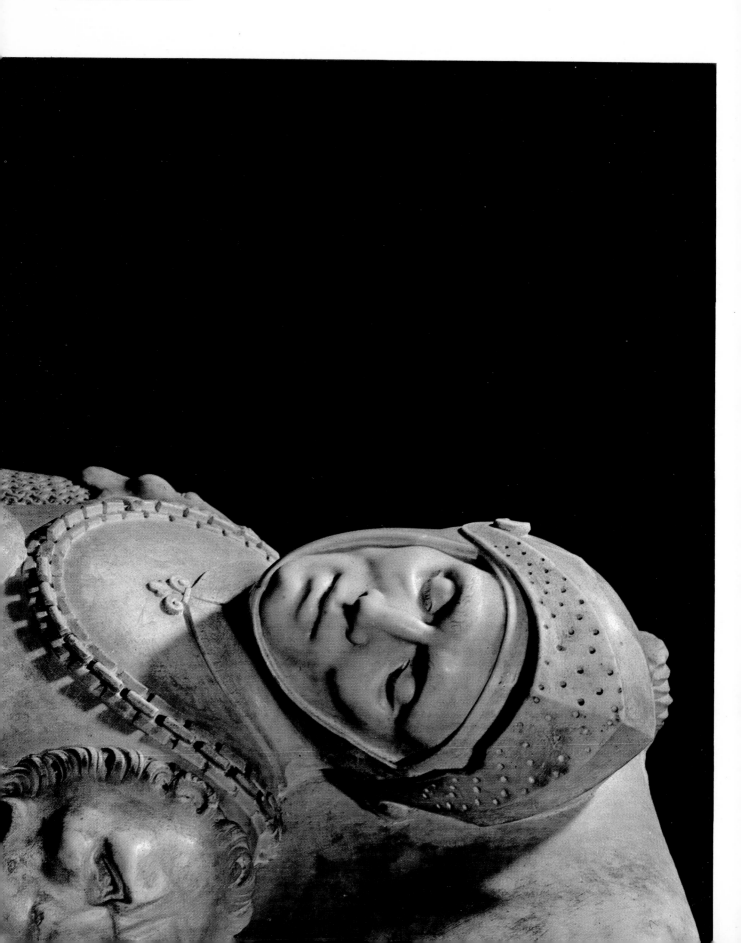

Santa Maria in Porto

Exterior

The Church of Santa Maria in Porto
is a large building, begun in the 16th
Century and finished two centuries later.
The façade, in two tiers adorned with statues,
has an academic dignity. It is the work of
Camillo Morigia, who also designed
the tomb of Dante.

Santa Maria in Porto
Byzantine bas-relief
with the Virgin

Tomb of Dante
Exterior

Tomb of Dante
Interior

Piazza del Popolo

This square is the civic and commercial center
of the city. Its present state reflects
the influence of the Venetians, who enlarged
it and, in 1483, erected the two columns
in front of the Civic Palace. The Palace
was rebuilt at various periods between
the 17th and 19th Centuries. To the left
of it is a portico built with
6th-Century columns.